Michael Jackson Speaks from Heaven

A Divine Revelation

Matthew Robert Payne

You can contact Matthew, read his blog, support his ministry or request a prophecy from Matthew at http://personal-prophecy-today.com.

If you send a private message to Matthew Robert Payne on Facebook, you can become his friend. He does not accept random friend requests from people he has no friends in common with due to scammers.

Cover designer: Akira007 from Fiverr.com

Editor: Freelance worker

The opinions expressed by the author are not necessarily those of Revival Waves of Glory Books & Publishing.

Revival Waves of Glory Books & Publishing
PO Box 596
Litchfield, IL 62056
United States of America
www.revivalwavesofgloryministries.com

Revival Waves of Glory Books & Publishing is committed to excellence in the publishing industry.

Published in the United States of America

Paperback: 978-0692724712

Michael Jackson Speaks from Heaven

A Divine Revelation

Matthew Robert Payne

Table of Contents

Dedication

This book is dedicated to my best friend in the world, Jesus Christ. I have conversed with him for thousands of hours, met him in visions hundreds of times, and he has stuck by me through all my days in the wilderness.

Acknowledgements

I want to thank everyone who contributed to producing this book. I want to thank the Holy Spirit for suggesting that I write this book. I want to thank Michael for coming from heaven. I want to thank my editor for polishing this manuscript. I want to thank my mother for loving me and supporting me in everything that I do. I want to thank all the people who helped me produce this book by supporting my ministry financially or requesting a prophecy from me.

I want to also thank all the readers who have motivated me to write this book. I hope you have the courage to write to me and tell me what you think.

I want to thank the Father and Jesus for making me into a person who will do anything that they ask of me. I couldn't have written this book if I wasn't taught by them and encouraged to be bold.

Foreword

Matthew Robert Payne has ripped down the gates of hell like no one I have ever heard of on this earth since Jesus and his disciples turned the world upside down. You will not regret putting Matthew on your radar and reading his books. The simplicity, depth and purity flowing from Matthew's spirit is very refreshing indeed. Listening to Matthew is like sitting with a grownup that has childlike faith. He can see, do and write the things that he does because he does not have a critical spirit. Instead, he walks in simple trust of the Holy Spirit and faith in Jesus.

This book will be, by far, one of Matthew's most controversial books to date. Like Matthew of the Bible, Matthew Robert Payne has the persona of the ox and the lion. He has battled through much opposition and hoards have come against him on the behalf of others. But Jesus has brought him through each time. I, myself, know what that is like.

You will be hard pressed to get through this book without being profoundly affected. Imagine heaven coming to earth. You can meditate on the words that Matthew's heavenly guest shares about what heaven is like. You might even desire to be translated there or have heaven manifest for you here. If you desire it with all your heart, anything is possible.

Your ideas of what heaven is like and who will be there might well be shaken, and that is a good thing. The systems on earth have their roots/design in heaven as Jesus intended. Though heaven is void of corruption, negativity and emotional hurt, I mention it here as this book will have an effect on your understanding of how things can be — as they are in heaven, so shall they be on earth one day. Why not today? This book is full of open-ended possibility and inspiration. I hope that you enjoy it as much as I did. Apply the grace that God has given to you, and you will understand how that same grace has been applied to and through Matthew.

A quote that Matthew uses all the time would be perfect to represent Michael as well, along with this book and all of Matthew's books.

"Life isn't about waiting for the storm to pass; it's about learning to dance in the rain" (Vivian Greene).

So come and dance in the rain. :)

Sheldon T. Bennett

Paramedic

Introduction

I am here with Michael Jackson. I have to say that just starting out and sitting down to actually interview Michael fills me with trepidation. Before I begin, I want to share with you that I have given about 20,000 prophecies from the Father and Jesus to people. For 20 years, I have been bringing messages from Jesus in the Bible to people.

I am very well versed and experienced in receiving messages through the Holy Spirit and through Jesus and the Father for other people. I have spent time receiving messages for the church in my country. I have been used in churches to deliver prophecies in a corporate setting.

Before this book, I have been used to interview 19 saints from heaven, and those interviews are included in the book called, Great Cloud of Witnesses Speak. When I wrote that book, I was very nervous, which made it really hard to write.

I knew that certain Christians would speak up and have some negative things to say about that book and tell me that it was wrong and that I was deceived and that it was not of God. Still today, people are complaining about that book, making accusations against me, saying that I was practicing witchcraft, being a medium and involved in activities that are not allowed in the Bible.

People tend to forget that Jesus spoke to Moses and Elijah on the Mount of Transfiguration. These were people that have passed on. Elijah had passed on to heaven physically without dying, and Moses had died. You'll remember the scripture in Jude 1:9 that records the dispute over Moses' dead body between the angel Michael and satan. Moses physically died, and Michael buried him.

Jesus shared in the scriptures that God is not the God of the dead, but he is the God of the living. Moses was definitely someone who had died and yet was alive in Christ in Abraham's bosom. He visited Jesus, and though it was uncommon, it was certainly allowed. We are also permitted to speak to the great cloud of witnesses mentioned in Hebrews 12:1, and when God wills it, it is possible to communicate with a person who has passed on and who is already in heaven. With all that said as an introduction, I just want to underscore at this point that I am nervous about releasing this book.

I am more nervous today because when I wrote Great Cloud of Witnesses Speak, I was interviewing people in the Bible that Christians would agree are in heaven. With this interview, there will be numerous disputes about whether Michael Jackson made it to heaven. People will wonder whether he was a Christian, whether he repented from his sins and whether he had accepted Jesus Christ as his Savior. All of those things are personal between Michael and Jesus, and God is the one who decides who gets into heaven.

I have seen an interview with Michael, and someone asked him what he thought of Jesus, and he spoke with such love and adoration as he answered that Jesus was always his friend. I remember his response in that interview, which was very convincing that Jesus was a real part of his life.

I did not need convincing. But some people, no matter how much proof I offer, won't be convinced, even if I were to include links to YouTube videos of Michael being interviewed about his faith.

I am not going to spend any time convincing people that Michael did what was necessary to go to heaven. I realize that there are some people that won't believe me, no matter what I say. I know that I cannot prove that Michael is in heaven. I know that at the end of the day, the words of this book and whether my visitor was, in reality, Michael Jackson, have to be weighed by each reader and accepted by faith if they are true or not.

This book is a result of a three-hour interview that I had with my visitor who, with all of my heart, I believe was Michael. Let the words that he has to share bring a conviction to you also, and may you share this book far and wide if you agree that I spoke with Michael.

Just before we start the interview, I want to mention that Kat Kerr, who has been to heaven at least a thousand times, has seen Michael Jackson there. If you are reading the paperback version of this book, you can search on YouTube under the title *"Kat Kerr Says Michael Jackson Is in Heaven."*

For those reading on a Kindle, computer or phone, you can simply follow this link to see what Kat Kerr says about

Michael being in heaven:
https://www.youtube.com/watch?v=j0dW3b58RDM

Question 1
Can you tell people how we met?

Well, that story is very interesting. You are a very unique fellow, Matthew, and you are a person who is open to the supernatural. You have often noticed that when you are talking about a person or when you are concentrating on a certain person, the person turns up in a vision. Many times, you have been talking about a saint from heaven to someone else on Skype, and that saint has appeared in your house. It's as though the saint that is being talked about wants to listen in on the conversation that you are having about them.

With that understanding, perhaps the readers can see that since you are open to the supernatural and since you operate supernaturally when you are concentrating on a certain person, the person will show up. After I died, you found out that I was preparing for a concert. I had made a film about my concert preparations called "This Is It" that included information about the rehearsals and interviews with me.

You were watching my concert and film on television. As I was singing and dancing to one of the songs, I suddenly materialized in front of you in a vision, similar to how people see a ghost. They see something in their imagination, and then it appears. I appeared in front of you, singing and dancing, and your first words to me were, "What are you doing here, Michael Jackson? You're the King of Pop."

You remember that my answer was inspired and obviously came from heaven. I answered you, "What do you mean, Matthew, by calling me the 'King of Pop?' You are good friends with the King of Kings, and he sent me to come and see you."

You will remember how that answer blew you away because one of the names of Jesus is the King of Kings, and he is so powerful that he will be recognized one day as the King over all the kings on the earth. One day, Jesus will control the earth and will be living on it, and there will be many kings on the earth, but they will all answer to him.

When I said that you are best friends with the King of Kings and that he sent me, it really resonated with you and stopped your arguments. You caught yourself wondering why such a popular person as I came to see you.

Your first reactions to me were of shock and surprise, probably how many people would honestly feel if I came to their house to personally visit them. You experienced some of those feelings, but my answer that the King of Kings sent me helped you understand how it was possible. I remember your extreme shock, and the answers that I gave helped reassure you that it was truly me.

That was one of my first visits with you. Since then, we have spent time together on a number of occasions. When I visited you, you had no idea that one day, you would write a book from an interview that I had with you. At the time, you were not supposed to know what would happen.

Sometimes, people want to know their future, and they become very curious about knowing what they will do in the future. Sometimes, Jesus can't share much about your future with you. Sometimes, the future is so magnificent, amazing and profound that if you knew about it ahead of time, you would run away from your calling like Jonah the prophet did.

We didn't tell you about the interview with me until about a year ago, yet for the longest time, it hasn't been on your mind. Just yesterday, a friend reminded you that they heard you speaking and saying that you would be interviewing me in the future. We reminded you that you would write the book and interview me.

For those who are interested, Matthew will also interview Steve Jobs from Apple; Lady Diana, the Princess of Wales; and Whitney Houston. You can keep Matthew on your radar and watch for these additional books in the years to come.

My interview is the first, and the others will follow. Matthew has met Steve Jobs a number of times. He has also met and dialogued with Princess Diana several times and has now met Whitney Houston a couple of times, including tonight when we kept him awake.

He will be prepared to interview them. It really all comes down to the questions that you decide to ask that allows the speaker to say what they want to say. Like I said, I have been prepared, and ever since I came to heaven, I have known that I was going to be interviewed by Matthew. It is good to meet your interviewer and know about him.

When you are popular and interviewed by certain people, such as Barbara Walters from "60 Minutes," as an artist, you should have an idea of the style and the person who interviews you. You should have an idea of what you will say and how you are going to frame your answers. You should decide how much detail and depth you will cover in the interview because you like and respect that interviewer, and you plan to put everything into the interview.

You might not know that we have movie screens in heaven, and we can watch the lives of certain people on earth, especially if we are going to influence them. You can watch the person's whole life on the movie screens and pay attention to the significant events that shaped the courses of their lives. Heaven is amazing as you can actually watch the entire life of the person in an hour. In earth time, you can watch everything that Matthew did in 49 years of life in just an hour of heaven's time.

It is like a tremendous documentary in high definition and great sound, and you really experience everything. You even hear the thoughts of the person before they do what they do and before they say what they say. I have watched Matthew's whole life and know everything about him — even more than he knows about himself.

The movie screens also play the future of the person. You can look at a certain saint, a certain person on earth, and you can play their future and see everything that they achieved on earth. You can watch everything that they do, and what they achieved, including every decision they made, both good and bad. You can see their whole future played out on that screen.

I am very aware of everything that Matthew has been through and of what sort of person he is. I really understand the true Matthew, not what people say about him but his true heart. I understand the true love, the compassion and the mercy that he has for others. I know his true intellect and his capacity for the things of God. I truly understand him.

I know what he will achieve and what this book and other books will accomplish. He is going to write over 50 books, and I know what they will achieve and how popular he will become around the world. Even though people mocked this book the year that it came out, in 20 years' time, they will not be quite so vocal. They will realize that Matthew is a true prophet and that he really does hear from God.

People will see that when God wants to bring an important message to the earth that he can use Matthew Robert Payne to deliver that message. Matthew has proven to God that he can be trusted to do whatever God wants him to do. This book is entirely heaven's idea. Matthew didn't meet me and decide to interview me in his own strength. That would really be madness and setting yourself up for mocking and unwanted abuse. No, this book was heaven's idea.

As I have said, Matthew and I have met a number of times. Matthew had a friend on Facebook who was one of my fans, someone that really loves me and was in love with me. At one point, when I was alive, she tried to contact me to meet me and was almost successful. A couple of times, Matthew was chatting back and forth with her on Facebook, and I turned up and chatted through Matthew and said hello to her. We had a wonderful conversation, and she was really happy.

We used that occasion for Matthew to experience more of me and to get to know me better. Every time that she started chatting with Matthew, I would turn up and have a conversation with her. I really blessed her, and she was really happy that Matthew could be used to be a conduit of conversation from me to her. She was really happy that Jesus allowed her to speak with me. We used those conversations for me to get to know Matthew better.

People do not understand that life is a lesson, and many things happen in your life for a reason. The suffering, the pain, the hardships, the good times, the good decisions, the bad decisions — everything that happens in your life is for a reason and a purpose. It is up to you to discover those reasons and purposes, and we have used everything on earth that Matthew has been through. See Romans 8:28.

His whole life has been a preparation for this interview. We have had various conversations and interactions, and every time that we met, led to him being comfortable to interview me at this time. God prepared him well for me to come here and be interviewed by him today.

Question 2
How do you feel about being here today?

I have to say, Matthew, that it is a tremendous honor to be invited to speak on earth.

This conversation today has been orchestrated by the Holy Spirit and Jesus, and the Lord placed it upon your heart and gave you instructions to follow. Because of that, I am here, and I am deeply honored to be a voice to speak to the people of earth. When I was here on earth, I had an amazing collection of songs, and for a time in my life, my accomplishments shone very brightly as multitudes of people knew me and loved me.

Lots of people love my songs and adored me as a person. I have come speak to these people. Of course, I can speak to anyone who does a search on Amazon and comes across this book. I have a message for every person who reads this book.

We eagerly expect the outcome of this book; we know beforehand; we have seen the results of this book before it has even been made available. We can see the future in heaven. We know all of the readers who are reading this book and those who are really, really skeptical.

We know the readers who are reading this book who are going to be positively affected by it and going to be impacted greatly. I have come down to speak to those people. I think that it is very important for you to have a record of what I said.

Sometimes, we think that we know a person. In some measure, you can know me through my songs and through some of the things that I have said. Yet many people may have all of my songs and not really know me.

The songs can have different meanings to different people. Sometimes, the meanings would have been clearer if I took the time to explain them all to you.

Today, I speak from who I am and the redeemed part of me. I speak as a person who is alive in heaven and who has been in heaven for a number of years. In this interview, you may get to know me in part, the real person, the person behind the persona. You will get to hear what I have to say in a little bit about who I am and about what is important to me. You will hear what I consider important for people to know and how people should live while they are on earth.

I am really enjoying my time here. Matthew, you had the idea to go to bed. You tried to sleep, and you were visited by a number of saints, including Mary Magdalene, Whitney Houston and myself. We all started chatting with you and kept you awake. You were then given the idea to go and put on some music because the Holy Spirit did not want you in bed tonight.

You were given the idea to go and play my greatest hits on YouTube. You do not have any of my albums, so you started to play my greatest hits. After more than an hour, you started to have a feel for where I was coming from as an artist as you listened to some of my greatest songs. Once you sat down on the couch, you were comfortable enough to start the recording.

I recognize that you are nervous about the reactions that people are going to have. Three kinds of people are going to read this book. Many people will really love this book and cherish it and read it more than once. They will rave about it to their friends.

Other readers will have mixed reactions to the book. They will have their doubts as to whether it was actually me speaking. They will read the book but not be fully convinced that I was speaking.

Other people will read this book and approach it with skepticism, and nothing that they read or that you say will convince them that it was me. These people might be very vocal on Amazon and give you bad reviews. You will have people email you, telling you that you are wicked and that God is going to punish you. Satan, who is a real entity, will use these people to try to upset you and try to annoy you and try to crucify you, like people crucified Jesus Christ.

You know that Jesus Christ came to the world, and he was a beautiful person — so sweet and full of love and compassion for people. He had a transforming and a profound message.

He was the best teacher who ever came to earth. Not only did he teach really profound things, not only did he have compassion and love people, not only was he the most amazing person to get along with, but he did many signs and wonders to prove that he was divine. He healed many people, walked on water and turned water into wine. He did many miracles, which should have convinced people that he was from God. He really did have a divine revelation for the people of earth.

Yet at the end of the day, he had these critics and haters. He had people who rose up against him and called him names. He eventually had people rise up against him and kill him.

That is because he was such a pure soul, and he was a gift from God to mankind. In a similar way, I was a pure soul, and many people said evil things about me and accused me of hurtful things. When it came to the truth of the matter, I was murdered because people in the music industry were not happy with some of the things that I was saying toward the end of my life. However, in heaven, we don't focus on the negative, and I don't want to share more details about my death.

I am very happy, and I felt really blessed to be chosen to come and speak. I am a little different from the saints of heaven who were interviewed before by you. They were true heroes of the Bible. My popularity on earth was enormous, which opened the door for this interview. God is going to use my celebrity status on earth as a draw for people to read this book.

Since I am so popular, people will be really grateful for this book. At the same time, many other people will accuse you of making up everything in this interview to make a great name for yourself.

Some people will not be convinced by this book, and many Christians will be outraged and express their negative views on blogs and posts about you, calling you a false prophet and false teacher. It is different for me to be here. Because I was such a popular person on earth, it is also humbling for me to come back. Not much footage or documented information tells what I feel about Jesus, what I think about heaven and what I think about what is important in the Christian life. It is a real honor to be invited here, and it is a real blessing from God.

Before I even lived my life, before I even came to earth, Jesus designed and planned for me to live the life that I lived and for me to one day come back to earth and share this message. In this way of looking at things, it seems that I lived my whole life and became so popular because God wanted to send this message to people. He wanted to reach certain people that the Christian church might not have the ability to reach. He wanted to use someone who could speak up for him and speak up about heaven and influence the people of the earth. In the story of Lazarus and the rich man that Jesus told, the question was raised about what effect it would have if a person came back from the dead. Today, many people have come back from the dead and testified about heaven. This is just one more way for God to reach people.

People who know me well will realize that it is me speaking when they get to the end. Some of the people who know me really well, those who are in my inner circle, will already know that I am speaking by some of the words I have used. Some of the things that I have said, along with my fundamental, simple language, will show them that I am speaking. More people will be hopeful at this stage that it is really me speaking, but some of the skeptics will already be convinced that this is a total sham.

The funny thing is that some of my most vocal skeptics spend the most time listening to my songs. They take my songs apart and say that they are garbage, say that they are not good and claim that they are hopeless. Some of the skeptics, no matter how opposed they are to the message, will invest the most time into trying to disprove the message. They will read this book a couple of times. One of the skeptics might even read this book, pick it apart line by line, take out the Bible and write another book coming against this book. They will try to show other Christians or people in general that this book was an evil fantasy and a deception. They will try and warn people to stay away from this book.

Madonna taught the world that no news is bad news. Any sort of advertisement is a good advertisement, and even bad publicity or negative events can promote a person. Matthew, you, too, will have some bad press, but you will have this book produced and published before the elections in the U.S.

I deeply respect and love the people who are skeptical of this message, and I hope that they share this on Facebook and on Twitter, making a lot of noise to everyone they know that this book is false and is deceptive. The louder they scream and the more noise that they make, the more that true, honest, loving and pure people will be drawn to read this book and be blessed by it.

You really have nothing to lose. All you have to lose is your reputation, Matthew. You are no one in the world. Since you are not an important Christian figure in the world's eyes, you have nothing to lose. Since you are not well known, you will not be hurt much by people calling you a false prophet or evil or wicked because you are simply doing what the Lord Jesus has told you to do.

You have known this interview was coming for a couple of years, and it is both my pleasure and my honor to be here and speak to you. I am so impressed that you have obeyed the Holy Spirit today and started this recording that will become this book.

It is interesting that you have written 17 questions for me to answer. Normally, you have no idea how long an interview will be. You have no idea how long I will speak. You have a computer, and you are just recording. After you complete the QuickTime recording, you will have this typed up.

You can easily carry the computer into the kitchen and take a drink of water to refresh yourself. You can easily speak, whether this takes an hour or two hours or however long it takes. You are quite willing to speak for as long as I speak, and I am quite willing to speak as long as I feel led to speak.

However, what I was told to speak is another thing. I already knew what I was going to say before I came to earth. I had already seen the questions that you were going to write today. We had already seen you sit down and write them out. I have been aware of these questions ever since I went to heaven, and I knew that you were going to interview me and what 17 questions you would ask. I am very well prepared to answer these questions.

I have the answers ready that I am going to give. If you are not a Christian, I am also led by the Holy Spirit. Just like when you speak in church on the behalf of God and when God speaks through you, he can inspire the words that you speak. You can encourage people with them. I am inspired by God with the words that I am going to use for my answers.

If you can believe it, they are coming from God through me and through me to you. I am very happy to be here, and we will finish question two.

Question 3
What is heaven really like?

What an amazing question. I am sure that a lot of people will want to know the answer. You do not have to be a born-again Christian to want to go to heaven.

The majority of people in the western world believe that they are going to go to heaven. Most of them think that you have to have done some pretty bad things to not go to heaven.

People believe that if you are essentially a good person, you will end up in heaven. Regardless of whether they go to church, whether they practice a religion or practice a Christian faith, most people believe in a heaven and in its existence, and they believe that their loved ones are in heaven.

People often say to each other at a funeral, "At least they are not suffering anymore and are in a better place." Very few people actually believe that death is the end and that there is no more existence. Most people would say that they believe in an afterlife and believe that their loved ones will go to a better and happier place.

I will be responding to this question from a Christian perspective because many people mistakenly believe that you do not have to believe in Jesus or have faith in him to go to heaven.

The reason that Jesus came to die on the earth is to provide forgiveness of sins. If everyone goes to heaven anyhow, he would not have had to die. Jesus had to die in such a dreadful way on earth so that he could provide a gateway to heaven for everyone who believes in him and follows him. If anyone could go to heaven without following Jesus, then his death on the cross would have been pointless. Therefore, a person has to reconcile with Jesus and have a relationship with him to be welcomed into heaven.

Jesus said, "I am the way, the truth and the life. No one comes to the Father (God) except through me" John 14:6 (New King James Version).

Jesus is the doorway, and I want to make that very clear to you, dear reader, that if you want to go to heaven, there will come a time in your life when you will need to enter into a relationship with Jesus Christ. I had that relationship with him, so I was sent into heaven. With that being said, I know that I could have possibly upset some people, but I have to be honest.

What is heaven like? First of all, can you imagine being in a place where there is no sickness? Can you imagine a place where you never get a cold, never get the flu and where you can walk up a hill without getting a cramp or sore legs? Imagine that you could actually bump into something or stub your toe without feeling any pain. There is no pain or suffering in heaven.

That aspect of heaven is so interesting. Can you imagine a world without suffering? Can you imagine a world without slavery? Much of the coffee and chocolate produced in the world is made by people who are in slavery — who receive no wages for working on plantations producing coffee and producing cocoa for chocolate.

While you are enjoying your coffee or your chocolate bar, you are doing so on the head and the blood of people who are in slavery. In the west, you do not think about that, and you put those hard thoughts out of your mind, but it is very real to those slaves who are working 15-hour days, getting beaten and not fed very much. Heaven is very real to these people when they find themselves in a place with no suffering and no hardship.

Can you imagine going to a place where everyone knows who you are? Everyone knows all of the good qualities about you. Imagine walking down the street and knowing everyone there like you know your best friend. Imagine knowing people's thoughts, their character traits and every good thing about them. You will know some people in heaven, like your neighbors, really well, but you will even have a really good idea about what type of people strangers are when you pass them on the street and say hello.

You just receive information about them as you walk by. People in heaven might meet each other for the first time but will know all of the good points and all the beautiful parts of the other person. They start from that place in the conversation, and they start to really learn more about each other as they speak.

You may have a few people in your life who actually know about you, but many people see your faults and your failings. People may know your good points, but they also know your failings. Even those closest to you might judge you and want you to change and want you to become what they think is best for you. If you let them, they might force their ideas on you, and many friends and family will try to conform you to what they want you to do.

In contrast, everyone in heaven is at ease with who they were meant to be. Everyone is beautiful and is becoming the best that they can be.

There is no sin in heaven. As a man, you can walk past beautiful women and not have lustful thoughts about them or think about having sex with them.

As a male, can you imagine walking through a place with stunning women who are dressed beautifully without any temptation to have sex with them? How peaceful would it be to be in a place with no lust — with no thinking about a perverted form of love outside of marriage?

In heaven, you are really known for who you are. No matter how many songs I produced and no matter how popular I was, very few people understood me or actually knew me when I lived on earth. Many people in my life wanted something from me. So many people were close to me just for what they could get. I had very few people in my life who actually just loved me for who I was.

In heaven, everybody loves you for who you are. Everyone knows your good points. Everyone is aware of what a beautiful person you are. You might not feel as if you are a beautiful person on earth. You might have things in your life that make you feel worthless and ugly and that you just can't seem to get on top of. No matter how many times you confess your sins, you might not ever be able to free yourself from feeling like a terrible person.

In heaven, you are not that person. You are not doing anything that brings you guilt, shame or condemnation. You can look at a beautiful woman and not burn with lust. You are a whole lot better in heaven, and you are the person who you wished you could be on earth.

In heaven, you might see someone walking down the street shining like the sun. There is tremendous glory and authority on them. You might recognize Moses since it's easy to tell who he is because of the way that he shines in heaven. Everyone knows his power.

Well, on earth, if a really important person walked past you, like the current President of the United States, you might have evil or jealous thoughts and think, "He does not deserve to be president, and he is a real jerk. He has done nothing for our country. I wish that I were in his position; I would do a better job."

You might have really negative thoughts toward a person who is achieving so much more than you on earth. In heaven, you will not feel jealousy. In heaven, you will not be upset because someone has it better or someone is more important or someone has more authority.

There is no jealousy, no envy, no depression and no sickness.

You can watch people on earth and truly be empathetic and compassionate about their life. You can feel their suffering and be sad for them. This empathy will then lead you to pray for that person. Because your prayers are perfect prayers in heaven, they are prayers that are inspired by God, so God will answer them for you. You know your prayers are going to be answered, which turns your sadness to joy.

Heaven is a raw, unique place. Many people assume that when you go to heaven, you are going to be riding on a cloud and playing a harp. They assume life is going to be boring, and you are just going to be singing to Jesus and worshipping God all day. Many Christians feel that all they are going to be doing in heaven is going to the throne room where Jesus and God the Father sit. If you are not a Christian, I'll explain something. When a Christian sings songs to God, they enter into a position where joy and peace saturate and overwhelm them, almost like an ecstatic state. Christians love this peace and joy, and often only feel it when they worship God at church.

Yet, a person can have that same peace and joy from God without singing to him, but very few Christians live a life where that is happening to them without them singing to God. Thus, they assume that they will be singing all the time in heaven.

Don't get me wrong. Visiting God, singing and worshipping in heaven is so powerful and full of wonder that it can hardly be explained in words on a page. Being in the company of tens of thousands of angels and scores of saints worshipping is really foreign to any experiences that you could ever have on earth. I find it really hard, even today, years after my death on earth, to enter the throne room without falling prostrate on my face and worshipping. The glory of God in that place is so powerful that many times, it simply makes you fall to your knees or onto your face.

It is especially beautiful to me to be called out by God in the throne room and invited to come and sit with him — to snuggle on his lap and have him speak comforting, life-giving words over you while people worship. It is so special that just the memory brings tears to my eyes. God has time for you, time to spend with you and to be personal with you, just like any father on earth, no matter how important or busy that they were. If you love to worship God, and you love to lift Jesus high, then you will have all the time that you desire to worship in the sanctuary.

When you come to heaven, God knows your purpose and design. He knows what you are created to do even if you never lived your dream on earth and even if you never achieved your purpose.

One Christian pastor and teacher, Andrew Womack, leads popular seminars and teaches on people's purpose in life and on how to find meaning in life. When he teaches on purpose, he asks people to come forward if they don't know the meaning of their life. He has regularly found that a large majority of Christians come forward and admit that they do not know their purpose in life. If this many Christians who are supposed to know God and who should have a good connection with him do not know what they are here for, how many of them are actually doing what they are called to do?

Now, some of them who do not know why they are here are actually fulfilling their purpose on earth. They are actually walking in their destiny, but they just are not aware that this is what they were designed to do. Many Christians do not know why they are here and are not fulfilling their purpose, which is really sad.

Paul spoke about the gift of salvation and the fact that we are created as a masterpiece on earth in order to do the great works that we were created to do while we are on earth.

Ephesians 2:8-10

God saved you by his grace when you believed. And you can't take credit for this; it is a gift from God. Salvation is not a reward for the good things we have done, so none of us can boast about it. For we are God's masterpiece. He has created us anew in Christ Jesus, so we can do the good things he planned for us long ago (New Living Translation).

When you get to heaven, God knows what you were designed to do on earth. If that job exists in heaven, then you will be doing that job because that is what you were born, designed and created to do. Many people on earth say,

"What is the meaning of life? What am I designed for, and why am I here?"

Well, these can be hard questions to answer, and many people on earth struggle with these questions. What is the meaning of life, and why am I here? The meaning of life is for you to do what you were born to do in a way that makes God happy and that glorifies his name.

I'll say it again since it is so important. You are meant to be on earth to do what you are created to do, in such a way that people praise God, thankful for you being on earth. That is the meaning of life. What you are born to do is what you were designed to do. God gives the normal person keys, ideas and hints about what they are meant to do.

However, many people do not pick up on these keys and hints. They do not understand how to find their purpose in life. In heaven, you immediately know why you were born. It might not be just one thing.

For example, Rahab in the Bible saved the spies and was herself rescued from Jericho. In heaven, she is a creative writer of fiction and is busy creating beautiful and exciting stories for people to read.

She also manages three popular restaurants there, where she is a chef, a cook and also serves as a hostess. She is busy creating food and making people happy.

She does not spend all of her time cooking but comes out of the kitchen to meet the people who are dining there. She has all of the best heroes of the Bible dine in her restaurants.

She may actually be in the kitchen, create the dish, cook the dish and then come out and sit down with Moses or one of the other heroes of faith as he eats the food and is blown away by the flavors and the perfection of the dish. She really enjoys herself. That is an example of someone in heaven doing what they are created to do.

In heaven, I am a singer and entertainer who records music. I am essentially doing what I was doing on earth.

I am also involved in motivational speaking in heaven about achieving your destiny and doing things with a spirit of excellence. On earth, I was a real perfectionist — if I did something, it had to perfect.

Not one song of mine was released without my approval and without me being certain that it was the best that it could possibly be. Matthew read one time that I recorded about 100 songs for each album that I produced. I then picked the best of the 100 and made the album.

The reason that I had so many hits and sold many successful albums was that for every album, I wrote 100 songs and worked on and performed the best ones until I got it right since I was a real perfectionist. In heaven, I not only record music for heaven, but I also teach people how to perform better and how to become a better person.

Everyone in heaven improves at what they do. On earth, if you begin to play the piano at a young age when you are 4 or 5, you will be giving professional recitals and playing solo performances in front of a great audience by the time you are 18 or 19. Your talent and your ability improved due to the thousands of hours of practice because you became better and better at your gift.

People wrongly assume that everything will be perfect because they are in heaven. Well, that is a crazy thought that you could just immediately be perfect. Where would the learning and the character development be in that?

When you get to heaven, you are no better at your gift than you were on earth. In heaven, you continue to practice, and you become better and better at what you do. When you have been there 100 years, you are extremely good with exceptional talent.

Matthew was at a Burger King restaurant having a hamburger. I came down and told him, "I had my first hit in heaven." He inquired about the hit, and I told him that every week, the people of heaven vote on the best worship songs. Everyone's songs are created and played there, and the people of heaven then decide which ones are the best.

Each song can get one of three scores: a ten, a seven or a five. Everyone rates each song. When the people vote on each song that they hear, the song that has the most points for the week wins. One week, one of my songs was voted the best song of the week. When that happened, I came down to tell Matthew.

In the music industry, the song at the top of the charts is the song that has been purchased the most often during that week. You cannot really fake bestselling songs because you would have to buy all those albums. Everyone in heaven votes on which song they think is the best. Since there is no jealousy, envy or positioning in heaven, it does not matter who you are. They are not voting your song number one because you are Michael Jackson. I am competing against people who love God and who have been musicians in heaven for 2,000 years.

Writing and recording a number one song in heaven is extremely hard to do.

In heaven, people celebrate other people's successes, so they held a formal dinner attended by Lady Diana along with all the important guests of heaven.

I was given an award for best song of the week. It is a real honor, and everyone is happy for you. Like I said, it is really hard to imagine the atmosphere of heaven because there is no jealousy. The person whose song was voted number two and the person with the number three song also received their awards, but they were not jealous of me. They were really happy that they received number two because they might never have received number two before. That accomplishment just makes them more determined than ever to write a song that would become number one.

I wish that I could recite the lyrics and play the music of my number one song in heaven to you, but Matthew is not musically inspired. Even though I could tell him the lyrics, I am not going to do that. You can wait until you get to heaven and listen to it to see if you like my song.

Heaven is a really unique place. Everybody in heaven has an extremely nice house, and you will call them mansions. Some people who, only wanted a bush hut or a very basic house, got what they wanted. They get the house that their heart desires. Not everyone has to live in a mansion.

In fact, some people live in apartments and really love them. They especially love the views from the high-rise buildings. Others live on the first floor in heaven and are happy with that as well.

Some people live on the hundredth story of an apartment building in heaven. The multi-million dollar apartments would cost about $20 million on earth. Your apartment is decorated according to your taste. For instance, if you like antique furniture of a particular style, your house will be exquisitely furnished with that particular style of antique furniture with all your favorite ideas and all your favorite concepts.

Heaven will read your mind when you are on earth. You may see a table in someone's house on earth that you think is really fantastic. If you don't want to copy your friend and buy the same table for your own house, when you get to heaven, you will have that table in your house.

For instance, Matthew was at a club about 25 years ago with a piano bar where you could just sit and have drinks and listen to someone play the piano and sing songs. Matthew used to go there, listen to music and listen to people play contemporary songs. This piano bar had a professional coffee station next to it with all of these sweets and desserts and professional baristas making coffee. Matthew thought that he would love to have a coffee shop in his own house with a professional coffee maker and a selection of sweets. He wanted to have a house one day that was so big that it could hold a coffee shop.

Matthew fantasized that if he were rich, he would have a coffee shop in his house and thought that would be great. He has been on visions; he has been on trips to heaven, and he has gone to his house, which has a coffee shop that seats about 50 people on the second story. It is filled with beautiful sweets and professional baristas, angels who work there, serving the coffee in his future house.

I have a professional studio in my house where I record a lot of music with my staff. Heaven has a music room with a recording studio where you can collaborate, mix and socialize with other musicians.

Good music comes from a combination of your own thoughts and other people's music. You need to have collaboration of the influences in your life. When you listen to the music of other artists, you get your taste and your style in music from them, and you write new songs from the influences in music that you admire.

Mixing with other musicians who you really admire and listening to them record and hearing their songs really benefits you as you record your own masterpieces.

One of the musicians that I rub shoulders with in heaven is Elvis. Elvis is in heaven, where he records music, and I had to compete against him along with other musicians.

Heaven also has contemporary music charts with songs about love and about different aspects of living life. Some of the songs are specifically worship songs about God and singing his praises in heaven, but heaven also has a contemporary music chart just like the non-Christian music charts on earth.

I have not won the best song yet in the contemporary chart, but I won on the worship chart. I was going after the worship chart because I wanted to show Jesus and all of heaven that I loved him. It was very important to me to write a number one song. My whole life changed so much. It is an amazing thing to meet your Creator.

The Apostle Paul said in the Bible that he went to heaven in 2 Corinthians 12:1-3. He saw things that he could not put into words because they were too glorious to speak about, including amazing experiences, such as meeting God and Jesus.

Matthew has another question later on that asks, "What is Jesus like?" You can turn to that one in the book if you like and read what I think of Jesus. This is particularly about heaven. Jesus is the center of heaven, and all of heaven revolves around him and his presence. The whole meaning of heaven is Jesus. He is the main part of heaven, but we want to concentrate on other aspects of heaven besides Jesus in order to give you an idea of what it's like.

Another aspect of heaven that you might not realize is that everything there is free. You can go to the movies in heaven and watch a movie that was written, directed, filmed and acted out in heaven. You can choose any one of hundreds of new movies that come out each week. You can enjoy popcorn, ice cream, a soft drink or a coffee while you are served at the movies in heaven.

The theatres in heaven are luxury theatres where you have a whole meal at your seat and enjoy it while you watch your film. When you go to the theatre, it is all free, and if you go to a restaurant before you go to the theatre, that is free as well.

When you shop for clothes, they have professional designers, trendy brands and all sorts of unique fashions in heaven. When you shop, you do not have to try the clothes on as the clothes will tell you if they fit you. You know your clothes as you pick them off the rack.

It is nice to actually put them on and see them on yourself in the store, though. You can pick up the best clothes in heaven. You can have a wardrobe with 1,000 outfits in it. It is really up to you.

In heaven, time is different from time on earth. Like I said, you can watch a movie of 49 years of Matthew's life in an hour in heaven. That gives you an idea of how time differs in heaven.

On the earth, 365 days make up a year. If you own 1,000 outfits, you could wear one every day for three years in earth time. Everything is free in heaven, so you do not need to pay bills. You have no rent, mortgage, gas, electric, cell phone, Internet, insurance, car payments or credit card bills. Heaven has no bills whatsoever.

Selfishness does not exist in heaven. You can go shopping once a week to buy clothes and buy the next week's clothes at the same time. You can just rotate your wardrobe or schedule your time however you like.

Because there is no selfishness or greed in heaven, people act differently there then they do on earth. Some people shop for free stuff all the time on earth. For example, they might join Facebook groups to get free Kindle books. Some people have hundreds of books that they never read, but because they were free, they downloaded them. This attitude does not exist in heaven.

Since everything is free in heaven, people don't need to behave that way. Selfishness and greed is no longer an issue, so people do not have to continually buy and hoard everything.

You can go out to lunch and then to a movie for two and a half hours. You can then drink coffee and eat cake and go to another movie. After that, you can enjoy dinner out and go to a concert.

Or if you prefer, you can go out for the evening to a restaurant, enjoy a nice meal and then go to a movie. Afterwards, you can go out for coffee and cake without stuffing yourself. Since everything is free, you can watch two movies if you like. Whatever you decide, you can enjoy your night in heaven.

Your whole life in heaven and everything you do is worship to God. Music plays continually through all of heaven. You are always in the presence of God, and you always feel peace, joy and love from him and for other people.

Heaven has just an amazing and unbelievable atmosphere. You really have to forgive the Christians who have hurt you. You need to forgive them for their misunderstandings of you and of the world along with the religious attitudes that some of them have had.

You really need to ask Jesus to reveal himself to you and to start to speak to you so that you can get to know him and accept him as your Lord and Savior. You really need to get to heaven because heaven is just an amazing and wonderful place.

In heaven, everyone works for a living and does what they are created to do even though they aren't paid. I had the bestselling hit in heaven for a week that topped the chart. There is a chart for the most popular song, too, but it's hard to understand because it is different from the charts on earth.

My song was voted the most popular song for the week. The next week in heaven, another new song was voted best song for the week. Heaven also has an overall favorite song in heaven, which relates to the earthly charts as the overall most-listened-to song.

In the second week, if my song was still the most listened to and most popular song, my song would stay on the charts as the most-loved song in heaven. My song stayed at the top of the charts for a while. It took some time for it to drop down and be beaten by another song. You have to understand that to be the most popular song in heaven means that you are competing against the best songs for the past 2,000 years. Some songs have been the overall favorite for hundreds of years.

Things in heaven are in more in detail and better than earthly understanding, but you just have to be there. For example, you do not get paid for work in heaven. Even though I had a bestselling song, I do not actually receive the funds from that song because the song is not sold.

I just receive the recognition and the understanding that I have written a tremendous song that has blessed so many people. Amazingly, the songs in heaven help people worship God. The more they worship God, the more ecstasy, peace, love and blessing they experience.

The more they worship the Lord, the more of a beautiful experience they have. I was really pleased that I could help so many people with this amazing and prolonged experience as they listen to my song more and more and worship the Lord. Since we all enjoy what we do, we are not paid in heaven.

When you really think about it, why would you need to be paid when you don't need money in heaven, and nothing costs money? Can you imagine not having to pay for things? Can you just imagine, for one moment, doing what you are designed to do?

You may not understand what that feeling is because so many of you on earth do not know what you are here for. You do not know your purpose.

Matthew is born to be a prophet. Matthew is born to bring messages from God, instruct people and teach people sayings of God. He is also born to be a speaker in churches and at events, which will change people's lives. He is also born to be a writer. As he records this book, he already has 15 self-published books. He will write more than 50 books in his life.

Matthew is very fulfilled since he is doing everything on earth that he was born to do. Matthew has a really good idea of what it is like to be doing what you are born to do. But so many of you reading this book have no idea of what you are born to do.

When I said, "Can you imagine doing what you are born to do?" some of you struggle with that. Just consider it for a moment. Imagine that you are doing what you were born to do.

Imagine something that you love to do. Perhaps you are a Christian, and you do not gamble, but imagine that someone bought you a lotto ticket and that you won $20 million. If you never had to work again in your life, what would you choose to do? How would you fill your time?

Now that you have $20 million, you can study acting and become an actress. You can go on auditions even if you need to study for years and put a lot of effort into getting into films. You could pursue that ambition if that is your heart's desire.

Imagine if you had enough money to live and support yourself really well so that you could choose exactly what you want to do. What you would choose to do likely provides a good indication of what you are born to do. It's that driving force within you, yet some of you don't know what that is. Some of you don't understand it, but I was born to be a performer and a musician, and I do that in heaven. Surprisingly, I am also used in heaven to encourage people and motivate them to achieve their dreams. But it really suits me because I would have liked to teach people on earth how to be good musicians and recording artists and achieve everything that the artist was supposed to do.

In heaven, you do what you are designed to do. You do what you are born to do, and you are aware of that as soon as you arrive in heaven. As you assimilate and adjust to heaven, you start to have an idea of what you are born to do and train accordingly to fulfill your purpose. Then, you spend time during the week actually working on what you love, doing what you are born to do.

When you are born to do something, you really enjoy it. Matthew loves writing and producing books; he really enjoys hearing feedback from people who are blessed by his books. The Lord provides money for him as he gives personal prophecies to people and derives an income from those. Since the Lord provides money through his personal prophecies to produce the books, he does not have to sell the books at a high price. Instead, he sells them at a reduced price on Kindle. He also gives them away for free as often as Amazon lets him.

Since he does not have to earn money from what he loves to do, Matthew is already living in the heavenly environment. He would quite happily be in heaven and not earn money from writing books and speaking. He would certainly enjoy going to restaurants, drinking coffee at cafes and going out to the movies. He would love going to concerts, writing fiction books and writing and directing films, among other things.

In his mansion in heaven, he has his own television and recording studio. He has his own office to write his books along with his own research and support staff that will be working with him.

On another note, heaven has many parks with all types of wildlife, dinosaurs, elephants and other earthly animals. Heaven has many animals that are not on earth.

Heaven has all sorts of parks, flowers, streams, rivers and seas. It has all sorts of places to visit and beautiful places to go. Heaven also has actual portals where you can go from one place to another place in an instant. You can choose to walk on a path or in the forest, or you can choose just to go through a door and a portal by being in a house one moment but going through a door to a portal so that you end up in your favorite part of heaven.

You can visit various places throughout heaven. You can travel by public transportation or by taking a walk or you can just think of a new place and suddenly be there. You can translate to the other place or immediately go through a portal. In heaven, you can catch a bus, drive a car or ride a bike to get places, or you can just think about the place and appear there. You can leisurely stroll for 10 miles down the street to a stream or a park, or you can just concentrate on where you want to go and appear in the park.

Traveling in heaven is instantaneous. You can travel the distance from the United States to England in a second in heaven. Oh yes, heaven is that big.

For those of you who enjoy food like I do, I have some things to say about how heaven operates. If you enjoy cooking or are willing to learn to cook at school, you can cook your own meals. You can host a dinner party at your house and cater it for hundreds of people. You can do all of the cooking yourself or bring in catering staff to help you with it.

The caterers come complete with people who help you design the menu and others who help you with the invitations and the RSVPs. Everyone you invite comes to your party, but they still send you a courtesy RSVP. When the day arrives, people will help you decorate your house, set tables and provide entertainment or to be a guest speaker. Even if your house is not be big enough for you to host a sit-down meal for a hundred people, your house will incredibly expand for the night with a ballroom to accommodate as many people as you like.

You will not need to wash dishes, utensils or cooking equipment in heaven. When you have finished your meal, all of the dirty plates, utensils, pots and pans, and everything you used to cook magically disappears and is put away for next time. If you have a big function, you will have wait staff and everything that you need on hand to help you.

Some people on earth love doing professional catering; others love interacting with people and serving as waiters and waitresses. Some people can be keynote speakers at functions; others are magicians, jugglers or good entertainers, such as professional dancers or musicians who play in a band. You can request any of these people to help you with your function, and they are most honored to do that for you.

When I had the best-selling song for a week, we held a function in heaven at a great ballroom that fit an innumerable number of guests in it. Lady Dianna was my guest speaker and a world-famous rock star from one the world's biggest bands of their time played music for the function. I'll let you guess who that was, or you can ask God to tell you. One thing I will tell you is that not many people thought that he ever repented and accepted Jesus as his Savior.

I hope this chapter has given you some reasons why you would like to come to heaven.

Question 4

What are you doing in heaven?

Matthew wrote these questions before he realized what my answers would be to the previous question, but I have some more to add. What I am essentially doing in heaven is recording music, spending time reading the Bible and worshipping Jesus and interacting with saints. I have been developing my relationship with God and Jesus and spending a lot of time drawing closer and getting to know Jesus and my Father more intimately. As my intimacy with God grows, that love translates into my worship songs.

I am recording music and also teaching people how to perform and be the best person that they can be. I also perform concerts and include some of my hits from earth and some of the earth's popular songs in heaven. I have learned to perform and play other people's covers, and I perform with the musicians who wrote the songs. I also go to concerts.

As I have said, I perform and record music in heaven. I pursue Jesus and my relationship with him, and I teach people how to be successful.

I can't stress enough how much of my time is spent pursuing Jesus. I read the Bible and books about the

Christian faith. I listen to people teach the Bible, which is still popular in heaven.

Universities and colleges have people who teach about the Bible and about the saints. They teach the meaning of the Bible, so I go to the classes.

I have a mentor in heaven who is my spiritual adviser. He is not someone from the Bible but is a past Christian who is also a musician who achieved a great relationship with the Lord while on earth. He is a very wise person, but he is not someone who anyone would know. He lived hundreds of years ago and was not known by anyone, but like Matthew, he had a tremendous relationship with Jesus.

He instructs me in music along with my faith in God. He mentors me, so I spend a lot of time listening to him and the speakers who he recommends. I spend a lot of time reading the books that he recommends. I research to find the answers to the questions he asks me. His first name is Mark, and he is just beautiful.

You can just call him Mr. Beautiful, and he is really amazing. I get emotional when I talk about it, but I really owe my first number-one hit to him. Without his influence in my life in heaven, I could have never achieved what I did.

This might be hard for you to understand because I was so popular on earth. However, it is very hard to compete with musicians who have been in heaven for 2,000 years. It is very difficult to write a song that is more popular than the songs that they have written because they have been working on their relationship with Jesus for thousands of years. I want to stress that competitions in heaven are not things that make us vain or puffed up with pride, but they are there to help everyone strive to be the best that they can be.

It came as a real surprise that one of my songs became so well known. It just proves that who you are on earth responds well to who you are in heaven. The work that you do on earth affects who you become in heaven. If you are a person who just went to church on Sundays but did not really obey the Bible or Jesus or put your faith into practice, you are going to have a whole lot of work to do in heaven. If you just used your Christian faith as a free ticket to heaven, then you will be busy trying to grow your faith. How successful you are on earth translates into how useful and successful you are in heaven. I had all of my earthly experience as a musician and how popular I was on earth for years so that I could speak to people in heaven about being excellent. I already had a very strong work ethic that has only become stronger from the influence of Mr. Beautiful in my life.

Question 5
Do all people go to heaven?

We covered this before, but I want to say the reason why the question is here is so that I can address this subject further. Lucifer, who used to be an angel, is real.

One day, he decided that he wanted to become greater than God, and he wanted the other angels to worship him rather than God. God kicked him out of heaven, and he actually became the entity that people call satan. On the day that Lucifer left heaven, one-third of the angels went with him.

Satan has a real agenda on earth. He wants to destroy the lives of people who have become Christians and make their lives hard, but he also wants to deceive and destroy the eternal lives of everyone who does not know Jesus. He wants to implement his agenda to keep people deceived and to keep them from knowing the truth.

The world might have an answer to cancer and even to AIDS. But these answers are hidden. Satan tries to hide truth so that he can keep people in deception.

You can eat healthy fruit and other natural, cancer-fighting foods, but the world does not have those answers. You just see a post on Facebook from time to time, but you don't see this information published in the media.

Some of the biggest truths in the world are hidden from everyone by satan and by his control of the media and the entertainment industry. His grasp is far reaching. One of his biggest lies is to let people think that "good people" go to heaven. They believe that if you are not a child molester or a murderer, then you deserve to go to heaven.

Well, that is all fine and good and that sounds like a good God would allow that. But what father would allow a child molester to look after his children? If you knew a child molester with convictions for molesting 50 children between the ages of 4 and 10, would you let him look after your children? No, you wouldn't. You would not let him influence your children or spend any time with them.

Well, God will not let wicked people or people who have sin in their life in heaven. The only way to get to heaven is to have your sins erased, to have Jesus, who was without sin, cover your sin. Jesus came as a perfect person to die and take upon himself the sins of the whole world. He came as a sacrifice to pay for man's sin.

You know, you can do different things in this world. You can do something wrong, and you can be forgiven by the person you hurt, but you can still feel guilty about that for the rest of your life. Nothing in the world, outside of the forgiveness of Jesus, will take away your guilt and condemnation when you do something wrong.

Jesus came to the earth to provide a way for people to be cleansed from their sin. They can pray to him and ask for forgiveness, and they can be given a sense of peace, love and understanding that they have been forgiven. They can make peace with themselves. Jesus actually came to provide a way for people to be forgiven for their sins so that they could clean up their act and become a better person and be allowed into heaven.

If Jesus has not forgiven your sins, if you have not asked Jesus to forgive your sins, that would be like the parent letting the child molester coming into their house to look after their children. God is not going to let you into heaven unless you have asked Jesus for forgiveness of your sins. The sad truth is that not everybody goes to heaven.

If you are not a Christian and you are reading this book, you might think that this is harsh. In John 14:6, Jesus said, "I am the way, the truth, and the life. No one comes to the Father except through me." Jesus was killed for who you are and to make a way for you. He is saying in that verse: "I am the way to heaven, and I am the truth, and I am the meaning of life. No one comes to God except through me."

Jesus was either lying, or he was telling the truth. Hell is a real place where people suffer for eternity. You have a choice. You can choose to accept that Jesus died for your sins, ask him for forgiveness and ask him to rule your life, or you can choose not to and take a chance of going to hell.

I understood the message of Jesus and his forgiveness, and I asked him to be my Lord, and I lived my life for him. Not many people knew about my beliefs as I had a very private life. I kept my faith close to myself.

I totally believe in Jesus and love him with all my heart. Some people do not go to heaven. One thing I can tell you is do not judge Jesus the way that you judge Christians. Go and get yourself a copy of the Bible and read the New Testament, especially the books of Matthew, Mark, Luke and John. In them, you will read about the person, Jesus.

You may have heard about Jesus from the church. You may have heard about Jesus in the media. You may have heard that Jesus married Mary Magdalene, which he didn't. You may have heard many misconceptions about Jesus. You may think that Jesus was just a good teacher. You may have all of these opinions. You can read about Jesus in the Bible and see if he is the sort of person that you would love to give your life to and devote yourself to.

I want to inform you that when you read those four gospels with an open mind, your opinions might change. At the end of this book, I included a prayer so that you can pray to accept Jesus into your heart.

Some people will reach out to Matthew. Some people on this earth are beautiful Christian people who understand Jesus, who will show you how to live a Christian life and who will show you how to live a life that is worthy of God so that you can prepare yourself for heaven. But make no mistake, not everybody goes to heaven, and you can take my word for it. I am not a person who tells lies.

Question 6
What is your message to your fans?

Many people looked up to me, held me in the highest esteem and really loved me. They loved my music and the songs that I sang. They loved the energy that I put into concerts. Many people really loved me.

Some people could read the lyrics of my songs and understand who I was. Many people listened to all my interviews and read them, along with my book and got to know me fairly well.

I have to say that I really thank you for supporting me. I really thank you for loving me, and I really honor you. Knowing that I have fans and knowing that people enjoyed and loved my music gave me a great deal of pleasure and made me happy.

But in the end, I was not happy with a lot of things on earth. If I were on earth now, I would have lived my life differently if I knew what I knew now. I would have spent more time pursuing my relationship with God.

It is really ironic that I am here, yet at the moment, I'm back on earth in Matthew's living room. I am getting a second chance on earth, and I am seeing things a little differently. I want my fans to know that one hour of time in heaven is like watching 49 years of Matthew's life. I can watch every event that happened in Matthew's life in real time on video, but I might only spend an hour in heaven's time.

I can spend time having a coffee or a meal with you, or I can spend time in your living room or in your mansion talking with you one on one. I could even come and perform at one of your functions.

Now, wouldn't you like me to do that? If you are one of my fans, if you are a person who really loves me, you would love to spend time with me, and I want to spend time with you. Make sure that you pray the prayer at the end of the book and that you pursue the Christian life. Follow after Jesus and make sure that you get to heaven.

Read books about how to find your purpose in life and how to fulfill your purpose. Give your life to Jesus, become a Christian and follow Jesus authentically in your heart. Ask him to lead you to Christians who are authentic and then go to the teachers they like and learn from them. Find out why you are here and pursue your destiny. This is my advice to you. I really would love to meet you; I would love to sit down and spend time with you.

Matthew respected me and liked my music, and he was interested in seeing documentaries. He was watching the movie about my life even though he was not particularly my biggest fan. He knew my music but had never bought one of my albums, so I do not consider him a fan of mine or a real follower.

The fact that I can come and speak to Matthew and spend time with him is not just for this interview. It is for you, the reader, also. I wound spend more time with you because you really loved and adored me. I would have a lot more time for you, perhaps, than even Matthew.

Give your life to Jesus. Give this book out to other friends and advertise this book on Facebook to people who love me and make sure that they come with you to heaven so that they can meet me. I can have concerts and come and out and meet and talk with you and spend time with you.

Question 7

What is your message to your mother?

You can never be too sure, Matthew, if this book is ever going to reach my mother. You are not too sure how I am going to pursue this. Regardless of whether you think this will reach my mother or not, I have a message here for her and for my fans and the people who will read the book.

A close relationship with your mother is good thing. It is a unique part of life. Some people lose their mother to death. Some people have a marriage break up, and they grow up without their mother. People sometimes suffer from not having a close relationship with their mother. When you have a mother who loved and supported you, it is a really precious thing.

I want my mother to know that I really adore and love her. I love all the special times that she took me aside and spoke to me and told me that I was special and that I could achieve anything. She really sowed a lot of hope, love and belief into me, and for that, I'm really thankful, Mom. I am really thankful for your role in my life, and I really love you. You gave me excellent support throughout my life.

I just want you readers to know that your mother is a special person. Your mother was chosen by God to sow into your life and build you up and make you into the man or woman that you are meant to be. Appreciate your mother. Respect and love her.

If you know my mother, make sure you pass this book along so that she knows that I love her, and I deeply appreciate her, and I look forward to seeing her when she comes to heaven.

Question 8
What is your message to creative people?

You have to be yourself. Many musicians and other creative people get their inspiration from God. Other entities, whether good or bad, might also inspire them. Books also influence people, especially writers. They share information from books they read, and they receive inspiration from God or another entity and then bring it all together to create good things.

Make sure that if you are a writer that you are reading a lot, not just Christian material. If you are a Christian, make sure you read fiction from a wide range of people. Make sure that you have a wide influence coming into your life instead of just a narrow influence.

Many Christians don't read books that are not from Christian writers. They have a narrow focus. This can harm them and negatively affect the way that they relate to people who are not Christians yet.

If you isolate yourself as a Christian, you should quit watching television, going to movies or listening to contemporary music because all of those are influenced from elements outside of the Christian faith. Some Christians have a very narrow perspective on life.

If you are creative or a musician, make sure that you buy albums from musicians who you really love and listen to them. Let their work influence you and enjoy it. Do your best to try and understand the musician and work out what the musicians were saying in the songs.

If the musicians have biographies, read them. If they give interviews, listen to those as well or read them. Find out as much as you can about the musician. Anytime the musician speaks, talks or is interviewed, read what they say so that you understand where they are coming from. This will help you get a handle on making your music, and the quality of your creative output will improve.

Always work on yourself personally and work on producing a better product. Work on improving the sound and recording quality of your music.

Matthew does not know a lot about music, so I cannot address this topic technically with him as I might with other people. If you are a writer, make sure that you polish your writing and go through your project so that your writing is as simple, clear and straightforward as you can possibly make it. Do your research before you write and find information that will help your readers.

Keep reading. Explore what other authors say. Look at their styles. Adopt their same styles into your writing, but make them your own. Let them fully influence you as you read their work. Be bold!

Read all different types of material — blogs, interviews, articles, books, non-fiction and fiction. Let yourself be fully immersed in the skills and the abilities of other writers.

If you are a fashion designer, study designs and other designers. Watch fashion. Be yourself.

If you want to act, study acting professionally and watch as many performances on stage as you can. If you want to be in the movies, immerse yourself in movies. Buy movie scripts and read them out loud with your actor friends and practice, practice, practice!

If you are a creative person, do not feel pressured into doing what people expect. Do not cave to the pressure of what you think other people would like. Be free to do what you like and to be creative like you want to be. Even so, sometimes you will need to earn money even if you don't completely agree with the project. However, don't sell your soul in the process.

Matthew produced two books about angels. He enjoyed writing them, and people liked them, and they sold well. His first book on angels consisted of stories, and he enjoyed sharing them. He did not present many lessons or much teaching in the book. He was somewhat upset that the people were only fascinated with angels and not fascinated with God.

In his second book, he made the effort to teach more and to instruct people about the things of God. He was more pleased with the final result since he included more teaching and lessons. Do not sell yourself short in your abilities.

Make sure that you earn a living and that you are able to put a roof over your head. But make sure that you create at least in part just for you. Part of your creation should fully express who you are.

You may be a recording artist with a recording contract. Make albums that the record company wants. At the same time, do not be afraid to release a private album that you fund with your own income that includes songs that you really want to release.

If you can't release other music that is not approved under the terms of the recording contract, wait until you are free of the contract and release it then. Do not sell yourself short and do not sell out to the expectations of others.

Keep your own soul and spirit intact so that you can be who you want to be. Do not sell out to money or what is popular or what others want. Matthew would not have written this book if he only did what he wanted to do.

This book was a request from heaven, telling him to write it. However, there were a lot of reasons for him not to obey and complete it. He will face negative feedback for this book. And yet, when Matthew really is listening to what I have to say, he is excited about this project and excited about my words.

Be obedient to God and led by him. Do what God puts on your heart. Matthew is happy even though it is going to cost him some hardship and trouble, and people will speak out against him. He is happy to be doing something that he likes to do. He is writing books, talking to saints and producing something that people will enjoy.

Once the book is edited, he will choose a cover that he likes, and he will look forward to the positive feedback from people who will truly be blessed by this.

Don't give away who you are. Keep part of yourself hidden and private. Make sure that you are happy producing what you want to produce without focusing on money.

If you have a choice between doing something that won't earn a lot of money but that will bring you a lot of satisfaction and something that will earn a lot of money but will cause you to sell your soul, make sure that you choose the one that will make you happy even if you don't earn as much money.

You have to do what you are meant to do. You need to do what you are born to do instead of pursuing money because money can be a god.

In Matthew 6:24, Jesus said that you can't serve two masters. You are going to love one and disrespect the other or you are going to disrespect the first and love the second. Then, he went on to say that you can't serve God and money. Jesus made a clear distinction between serving God as your God or serving money as your god.

When it comes to being creative, you need to decide what is best for people, what is best for your soul and what is best for your personal self-esteem. Then, do what is in your heart to do, and do not let money be the deciding factor in your decisions because money is not God. God is God.

Jesus said to trust God to provide for you and not to fret in life. Right after Jesus instructed us not to serve money, he said these comforting words:

Matthew 6:25-33 (NLT)

"That is why I tell you not to worry about everyday life—whether you have enough food and drink, or enough clothes to wear. Isn't life more than food, and your body more than clothing? Look at the birds. They don't plant or harvest or store food in barns, for your heavenly Father feeds them. And aren't you far more valuable to him than they are? Can all your worries add a single moment to your life?

And why worry about your clothing? Look at the lilies of the field and how they grow. They don't work or make their clothing, yet Solomon in all his glory was not dressed as beautifully as they are. And if God cares so wonderfully for wildflowers that are here today and thrown into the fire tomorrow, he will certainly care for you. Why do you have so little faith?

So don't worry about these things, saying, 'What will we eat? What will we drink? What will we wear?' These things dominate the thoughts of unbelievers, but your heavenly Father already knows all your needs. Seek the Kingdom of God above all else, and live righteously, and he will give you everything you need."

Question 9

What do you consider important in life?

One of the most important things in life is to find out why you're here and to find your purpose.

Another thing that's important in life is to be in touch with your Creator and to have a knowledge of him and an understanding that you are a created being. You're here to make God happy and to do such a good job in life that people exclaim, "There must be a God!"

It's important in life to do what you're created to do. When you do what you're created to do, that will bring happiness, peace and joy into your life.

You may not be an artist or a musician who earns a lot of money. You may not become the most popular musician in the world. You may simply play a few gigs with your band, record an album that you love, advertise through Facebook and sell a few hundred copies of the album.

But then, you might receive feedback from a few of your friends or others who listen to it and who really appreciate your songs and what you've said. That's what's important. Being the most popular person in the world is really overrated.

As a person who was very popular, I had a hard time going from place to place and having privacy. People flocked to me everywhere I went, which made my life a logistical nightmare. That was one of the problems of being so popular.

I was also involved with people who were truly evil. I wish that I hadn't been involved with those wicked people in the music industry who eventually killed me. I wish that I hadn't spoken out against them.

Sometimes, I wish I were still living on earth and still producing albums, doing concerts and bringing joy to the people of the world. The answer isn't money. Choosing success and money and what the world considers success isn't your best bet.

Your chief purpose in life should still be to do what you are born to do and what brings you satisfaction. Do what honors God and helps you intimately know him and Jesus. This should be your chief purpose in life. You should pursue God and an intimate relationship with him and Jesus. You should pursue what you are born to do here.

Of course, family is very important along with spending time with your loved ones. Your family is an important aspect of life on earth. I do miss my family and my children, and I am constantly looking over them and praying for them.

Being loving to all people and treating others with honor and respect is a really important part of life. It's important to be a good father and a good husband or wife to someone.

Question 10

What would you say to Christians?

First of all, I'd like to say to Christians, "Get to know Jesus."

Matthew has a book called Finding Intimacy with Jesus Made Simple. In that book, he's received a lot of revelation about the life of Jesus that's not recorded in the Bible. It's revelation that the Holy Spirit gave him.

Read that book. The book is usually free on Amazon or ITunes. "Buy" a copy of that book and get to know Jesus.

Pursue Jesus with all your heart. Both Matthew and I share this important message to Christians. The Bible says the following:

1 John 2:15-17 (NLT): "Do not love the world nor the things that offers you. For when you love the world you do not have the love of the Father in you. For the world only offers a craving for physical pleasure and craving for everything we see and a pride in our achievements and positions. These are not from the Father but from this world. And the world is fading away along with everything that people pray. That anyone that does what pleases God will live forever."

That's my message to Christians. Do not love the world, and do not love what it offers you. Instead, deny yourself and pursue God with all your heart, pursue your purpose in life and achieve that purpose with the help of God. Jesus said this in Luke 9:23: "Then He said to *them* all, "If anyone desires to come after Me, let him deny himself, and take up his cross daily, and follow Me."

The way to living a victorious Christian life is through self-denial and denying yourself certain pleasures and expenses that you don't need to spend your money on. Instead, choose to pursue God with your finances and support other people and their ministries.

God would prefer it if you were to spend a lot of your time pursuing him and what he wants for you instead of pursuing what you think that you want. Get to know what he wants you to do in your life and do it with all of your heart.

Question 11

What have you got to say to skeptics of this message?

First of all, as skeptics, you are needed to properly advertise this message and to properly get this message out there; you are needed.

Every book that has negative reviews on it is an authentic book. Some books have only five-star reviews on Amazon. You have to wonder, "Did everyone think this book was fantastic?"

So many people oppose Jesus Christ. Instead of honoring him, they use his name as a swear word.

People not only use "Jesus" and "Jesus Christ" when they swear, but they actually write those words in fiction. They write them in stories, and they swear with his name in writing, which they actually had to intentionally include in the book as swear words.

People are so upset with the Christian faith, which is one of the reasons that they actually use the word "Jesus Christ" as a swear word. In Matthew 5: 33, 34 in the Sermon on the Mount, Jesus said that Jews previously took God's name in vain, but he told them not to swear.

Jesus can live with people using his name in vain. He has broad shoulders and can live with skeptics and with people who hate him.

However, he isn't too happy with people who claim to be Christians but then don't act like Christians, people who claim to be Christians but who then don't do what he taught. Jesus doesn't like that behavior as they bring his reputation into disrepute.

When a Christian speaks out against another Christian or acts unloving, Jesus does not like that. If someone reads this book and then goes to a great effort to insult and abuse Matthew, Jesus will not be pleased. Matthew was very happy to produce this book because heaven instructed him to do it.

What I would say to the skeptic is pursue Jesus. Get to know him and who he really is.

Discover Jesus in the gospels of the Bible — in Matthew, Mark, Luke and John. Discover his personality and then really get to know him. Really study him and then come back to this book and see if I've said anything contrary or different than what Jesus would have me speak. I might speak about many things that are mysteries to you. But they should lead you to honestly seek God for clarification and peace. A lack of understanding does not give you the right to attack someone.

You'll find that if you're a skeptic and if you're a person who speaks out against this book or speaks out against the Bible, there's something in the message that offends you or something that you don't like or understand or that you don't agree with.

It doesn't mean that you're right. It just means that you're offended and that you've got an issue with something that I said. That's okay! You have a free will. You have the right to be a skeptic.

Advertise this book on social media and tell people, "Come and see the biggest false prophet that's ever lived. He thinks that Michael Jackson is speaking; check out this book."

Do your best to negatively promote this book, and I pray that you will really get to know Jesus and his character. I pray that your mocking of this book and your attitude toward this message won't affect your entrance into heaven. I pray that Jesus will forgive you.

Question 12
What is Jesus like?

Imagine meeting the person who created you. Imagine meeting the most loving person that you could ever meet. Imagine looking into a person's eyes and knowing that he sees right through you, but all you see in his eyes is love and acceptance.

Imagine a person that could look into your eyes who sees none of the wrong that you ever did but only sees the positive. He only sees your strengths and your abilities and your capacity to do good.

Imagine meeting a person who only speaks beautiful things to you and who encourages you to be a better person than you are. Imagine looking into the eyes of fiery love.

I tell you, Jesus looks into your eyes, and you're just in love. You're just overwhelmed with peace, love and joy coming from his eyes. You're just overwhelmed with the compassion and the love that he has for you.

He has so much compassion. He really, really, **really** cares for you. He truly loves you.

He even loves the skeptic and the person who's going to totally trash this book. He doesn't like the behavior, but he loves the person. He's just has such a capacity to love.

The children flock to him in heaven. He walks around, and the children are hanging off him. He just loves them, spends time with them and really blesses them. Many children are in heaven because of abortion. Heaven has a lot of children.

When Jesus walks through heaven, people stop him to talk to him. He's got time for everyone. Jesus has time to spend with everyone. He will sit down and talk with you and eat a meal with you and hold your hand.

Jesus can actually be in two places at once and interact with two people at the same time. That is a bit mind-blowing and hard to understand that both people can experience the same Jesus at the same time. Even if time were a problem, Jesus could still minister to two people at once in two different places.

Jesus has the Father's eyes. The whole of the universe is in his eyes. You can actually see the universe as you look into his eyes.

He has unending wisdom and knowledge. When you talk to him, you know that he knows everything. He's a human, but he's got a God-brain and intellect.

He can listen to the prayers of a million people at once and take those prayers to his Father and add to them as he answers them. He can have a thousand different conversations with people on earth at once and yet talk to you while looking into your eyes and giving you his full attention.

He makes you feel special. He makes you feel like you're the greatest person alive. Every person in heaven that meets Jesus thinks that they're wonderful, knows that they're loved and knows that they're accepted. He has so much love.

He doesn't look at you through the lens of your mistakes or the bad things that you have done. He doesn't even remember the bad things that you've done. He just loves you. He really, really loves you.

It says in Psalms 103:12: "As far as the east is from the west, So far has He removed our transgressions from us." When you read this verse, you know that the east and the west never meet, so it seems a bit theoretical. But when you meet Jesus, you know it's real. You know that your sins are forgiven and forgotten.

When you meet Jesus, he's such an amazing individual. He's the center of heaven, and he's the crown of heaven. The whole of heaven revolves around him. The whole reason that heaven and the whole world exist is because of him.

He gives people free will and gives them the ability to hate him. He gives them the opportunity to speak out against him. He gives them permission to be skeptics and to trash this book. He still loves them.

He's disappointed with their choices, but he still loves them. He loves you regardless of what you think about this book. He still loves you. He loves you, the reader, who is really enjoying what this book has to say. He really loves you.

He has a paradise in heaven made for you. I know that I have said a lot about heaven. He has a place and a mansion and a perfect life designed for you if you choose to give your life to him.

Since even before you were born, he has a world that's designed for you with a place that you will love and really enjoy. He created it all for you. He designed heaven so that everyone there is happy.

If there are things that you want created in heaven when you get there, he'll create them for you. Better yet, he'll allow you to create them. Heaven custom creates what you desire. People in heaven are constantly creating things.

Jesus is a person who will give you everything that's good for you and everything that you desire. Even when you're on earth, he allows you to do things that he doesn't approve of, but he'll work those things out in your life so that they still turn out for your good. Romans 8:28 says it like this: "And we know that all things work together for good to those who love God, to those who are the called according to His purpose." He's just so amazing.

I loved him so much when I was on earth and understood him so well, but it can't even compare with how much I know him and love him now. He's just amazing. He really is the answer to everything and for everyone. I hope that you can come to know him.

Get Matthew's book, Finding Intimacy with Jesus Made Simple, and get to know Jesus. He has another book called Jesus Speaking Today that talks about what Jesus spoke as Matthew documented it.

Jesus speaks through other authors as well, and you can get to know him through these books, too. The book, Jesus Calling, by Sarah Young also really blessed Matthew, and he enjoyed that book as well.

Question 13

What do you say to people who are misunderstood?

In this world, people have no idea of who you really are, even your own mother. Sometimes she doesn't realize your full potential and doesn't know how popular you can become or how successful you can be.

Even with all my success on earth, my own mother knew me well but has no idea of what sort of person I am now, what sort of abilities I've got now and how successful I am now. She would have never considered how wonderful I have become. Even my own mother, who I loved and who loves me dearly, could easily misunderstand me.

Adultery is clearly sin and hurts many people, including the person who commits it. However, everyone has some type of sin in his or her life. It's easy to judge people when you don't have all of the information. They may see that you are caught in an adulterous affair and think that you don't love your wife.

They don't realize the temptation that you experienced and your repentance after you fell. They don't see the tears that you cried. They don't understand that, like David, God still calls you "a man after his own heart."

All they see and all they judge is the infidelity. They only see your mistake and the sin.

They judge you as untrustworthy and undeserving of any respect. They stay stuck in the past, even when you, your wife and God have moved past your fall.

People read magazines and get their information from the Internet or television. They make a decision on how they're going to react based on what they read and see.

If it's something that's controversial or if they don't believe it and if it's questionable, they make a judgment. They decide whether they're going to believe it or if they're going to reject it.

If they decide to reject it, they want to feel justified in doing so. They'll build a case for rejecting it and why they believe they are making the right decision.

People will reject and misunderstand you and then build a case as to why they're rejecting you. They want to justify themselves and label themselves as loving. They want to feel that they are right for misunderstanding you and judging you.

The world that you live in is full of misunderstanding and judgment. You've just got to learn who you are. You've got to know your good qualities. You've got to understand what's good about you.

One good way to learn the qualities that God loves about you and values in you is to receive a prophecy. If you search for Jeremy Lopez on Google, he can provide you with insight.

You come to realize who you really are and what your good qualities are when you understand who you are in Christ.

Matthew's got a book called "Your Identity in Christ," which talks about who you are as a person, as a Christian.

If you come to understand who you are in Christ and the truth about yourself, you won't be affected as much by what people say to you and about you.

When they misunderstand you, you have got to come to a place where you are very confident in who you are and what you stand for. When you reach this place of confidence and when you are actively doing what you are born or created to do, then people's misunderstandings affect you less.

Question 14
What are some tips to life and success?

We have covered some points about this topic, but I will add a bit more for clarity. First, get to know Jesus intimately as your best friend. Now, the process of becoming his best friend won't happen in six months. It will take you many years to grow into a deep relationship with him. That is one of my keys to success. Get to know your Creator.

When you buy a car, it comes with a handbook that describes the car itself and the car's workings. It provides a basic understanding of how the car operates.

If you went to the car's designer and had him show you videos with everything about the car, you could probably spend 40 hours listening to every technical aspect of the car. The designer of the car will tell you much more about the vehicle than that handbook.

Well, Jesus created you. You might think that your mother conceived you via sexual intercourse, but the ability to produce life comes from God. All life comes from Jesus.

Life does not just happen. As much knowledge as scientists have, they cannot create life out of something that is dead.

Jesus created you, so he is the one who knows why you are here. He is the one who knows your good qualities. He is the one who created you to be who you are meant to be. If things have gone wrong in your life, he is the one who can help you correct them so that you can become the person who you are meant to be.

The second key to success is to find out why you are here. Research what you really want to do to find out more about your purpose. Ask a prophet why you are here. He may ask you some questions and tell you why what he thinks your purpose is. If you give him some choices of what you think that you are meant to do, he can tell you what God wants you to do.

You can do multiple things and be happy and still do what you are designed to do. You have choices. Make sure that you love God and make sure that you love other people. It is better to have a great relationship with God and to be able to express love for other people unconditionally.

Now, some people who are not Christians do a wonderful job of loving others. I am not saying that you cannot love without Jesus in your life because love is something that God created in us, and we are born to love naturally. Everyone has the ability to love others. It is just that exquisite forms of love, the highest forms of love, are found in having a rich relationship with your Creator and having a spiritual aspect to your life.

Pursue God. Pursue a relationship with Jesus. Find out what you are born to do. Pursue love and do your best. Put your effort into pursuing loving relationships with everyone you know.

Question 15

If you could change one thing you did, what would it be?

I would have made some different choices regarding my connections with evil people. I would not have gone to bed with the Illuminati, who controlled major portions of the music industry.

I would have made the decision to work independently of them. I am pretty happy with what I achieved on earth. I am very happy with what I have achieved in heaven.

It's good to look at life with no regrets, so this is an important question. I would have spent more time pursuing Jesus. I would have put more time into my relationship with him.

A lot of people say that they don't have time to do things, but it is really a matter of finding time. I would have found the time in my schedule to pursue Jesus, to get to know him better and to have a better relationship with him. I would have more hits in heaven by now if I had known him better before I went to heaven.

I would have not pursued certain evil people in the music industry. When you get in bed with them, you do not realize how evil they are until their true colors emerge. As I have already said, I would have spent more time on my relationship with Jesus.

Question 16
What do you think love is?

Love is one of the most important emotions that we can feel.

It is one of the most important emotions in the world. 1 John tells us that God is love. How amazing to understand that the essence of love is really God.

You might not have heard that if you are not a Christian. You might not be familiar with the scripture that says that God is love and that might motivate you to actually get to know God.

Here is another scripture that I will share that most people who are not Christians may not know. You might have heard it at a wedding. 1 Corinthians 13:4–8 says,

"Love suffers long and is kind; love does not envy; love does not parade itself, it is not puffed up; Love does not behave rudely, does not seek its own, is not provoked, thinks no evil; it does not rejoice in iniquity, but rejoices in the truth; it bears all things, believes all things, hopes all things, endures all things. Love never fails."

I could go into great detail about what each section means, but you could search that passage on the Internet for a good explanation of what love is. So many songs sing about love, but they never seem to capture the full essence of what that passage says. A different rendering of that scripture that sheds another perspective is in the New Living Translation.

"Love is patient and kind. Love is not jealous or boastful or proud or rude. It does not demand its own way. It is not irritable. It keeps no record of being wronged. It does not rejoice about injustice but rejoices whenever the truth wins out. Love never gives up. Love never loses faith. It is always helpful and endures through every circumstance."

That is what love is. Love makes a man and woman fall in love together. Love is the foundation of families as a mother and father meet each other and have children.

Love wants the very best for each other. Paul described love for you. That verse, even with the help of the power of God, is quite hard to live out in your life. It is a good standard to follow.

Love is the inspiration for many, many songs. The music industry would have a real void if musicians did not write songs about love.

Question 17
What final things do you have to share?

Okay, I want you to know that all have sinned and fallen short of the glory of God, as it says in Romans 3:23.

I want you to know that you can be good as a person but not make it to heaven. The answer to heaven is Jesus. Like I said, Jesus told us in John 14:6, "I am the way and the truth and the Life, No one comes to the Father except through me."

Jesus said that that he is the way to heaven. He is the way to life. He is the truth of all existence, and he is the life.

He is the one who gives meaning to life and sustains it on earth. There is no other way to God the Father. There is no way to heaven except through Jesus.

As my final words, I want to share with you that I would really love for you to meet me. I would really love to visit with you on earth someday. If you enjoyed this book, you really need to do yourself a favor and read the Gospels of Matthew, Mark, Luke and John. Get to know Jesus.

Matthew wrote a book called The Parables of Jesus Made Simple. If you read that book, you will understand some of what Jesus taught in the stories that he told. His book, Finding Intimacy with Jesus Made Simple, will give you more of an understanding of Jesus' life and how to live the

Christian life. You can also learn more about Jesus in Jesus Speaks Today, another of his books.

As you come to understand Jesus and come to love him for who he is, your life will move forward on the right track. When you form a relationship with Jesus and pursue him, you can also learn your life's purpose and then pursue it. When you are loving to your family and to others, then you will be doing really well.

It has been my honor to be here and speak to you. I really wish that I could share my thoughts in another book and that we could speak again. I hope that Matthew writes another book in the future with 15 more questions.

I am afraid that no matter how long this book is and that no matter what questions were asked, that this book still won't answer all of the questions that you have for me. That is truly a shame. The questions were designed in heaven, and I answered them faithfully. I personally want to share with you that I would love to meet people from all walks of life.

Matthew is going to end this now and write our closing thoughts to the book. He will send this off to the typist and have it typed. Then you will have the book in your hands. God bless you, and I will see you in heaven.

Closing thoughts

I have to say that it feels very strange to go through a text and edit it to make it clear for a book when the words are not yours. For the past two days, Michael has been with me in my house as I went through the typed text, corrected what was wrong and clarified other points.

I am sure that some people might have read this book and been disappointed. I cannot do anything about that. It seems very evident that Michael is busy in heaven.

His thoughts on the meaning of life greatly interested me. I was also fascinated with his heavenly mentor Mark, Mr. Beautiful. I was impressed with the fact that Michael is also helping people to achieve excellence in heaven.

Some will mock this book, like any divine revelation, yet it cannot be said that Michael didn't stress the importance of knowing Jesus this side of heaven. I am impressed by his simple language and by the fact that heaven chose me to bring his voice to earth. I hope that you read and reread this book and listen to what he said, especially if you are not yet a Christian.

It was a joy to interview Michael, and I have enjoyed the process of polishing this material for publication. I did not know a number of things in this book before I wrote it. This material was taken from one, three-hour interview with Michael with one recording. Apart from minor grammatical corrections, this is the best format that we could provide for you to read.

As mentioned, I am going to include a prayer that you can pray if you want to give your life to Jesus and become a Christian. Here is the prayer.

Dear God,

I am new to praying. I don't know everything about Jesus yet, but Jesus is the kind of God that I want to have in my life. I believe that Jesus came to earth and died for my sins. I want to confess that I am a sinner and that I have done things wrong in life. I would like to ask you to forgive me for my sins though the sacrifice that Jesus provided for me. Jesus, please save me from my sins, and please send your Spirit to come and live within me as I try my best to get to know you and follow you for the rest of my days.

In Jesus' name I ask,

Amen

If you prayed that prayer, I would like to hear from you. Please write to me at survivors.sanctuary@gmail.com and let me know about your decision.

If you don't hear from me within a day, your email likely got lost. Please go to the contact form at http://personal-prophecy-today.com and send it to me so that I can get in touch with you.

I'd love to hear from you.

Email me

One of my biggest joys as a writer is to hear from readers who have enjoyed my books. I would love to hear from you if you liked my book. You can write to me at survivors.sanctuary@gmail.com and let me know what you think.

Write a review on Amazon

One thing I really love to do is to read the reviews of my books on Amazon. If you have enjoyed this book, you can really bless me and other potential readers by writing a candid and honest review. I take the time to read all of my reviews and will always respond and say thanks for writing the review. Even if you aren't comfortable emailing me, it only takes a few minutes to write a review. Please consider doing that for me if you enjoyed this book.

Support me

I spend a lot of my time writing books, and it can be quite expensive to have a book edited with a nice cover and the related costs of self-publishing. One way that you can support me is to make a donation to my book-writing ministry. You can support me at http://personal-prophecy-today.com/support-my-ministry/.

Request a personal prophecy

If you would like to request a personal prophecy or message from God, and you are not yet a Christian, you can do so at my website. You will need to fill out a message in the section called "Note to seller" on PayPal, telling me your name, your gender and the fact that you are not a Christian.

If you are a Christian and you want to request a personal prophecy, please fill out the "Note to seller" on PayPal and include your name and gender. You can request your prophecy at http://personal-prophecy-today.com/request-a-prophecy/.

You can also check out my other books and blog at http://personal-prophecy-today.com.

Send me a friend request on Facebook

You can also send me a message on Facebook at my name, Matthew Robert Payne. Please send me a message first if you want to be a friend and if we don't have any friends in common. I don't accept friend requests from people if I don't have friends in common with them. I have found that there are too many scammers.

I look forward to meeting you in any way that you choose to contact me.

Other Books by Matthew Robert Payne

The Parables of Jesus Made Simple

The Prophetic Supernatural Experience

Prophetic Evangelism Made Simple

Your Identity in Christ

His Redeeming Love - A Memoir

Writing and Self Publishing Christian Nonfiction

Coping With Your Pain and Suffering

Living for Eternity

Jesus Speaking Today

Great Cloud of Witnesses Speak

My Radical Encounters With Angels

Finding Intimacy With Jesus Made Simple

My Radical Encounters With Angels - Book Two

The Beginners Guide to the Prophetic

Coming Soon:

Mary Magdalene Speaks from Heaven

Conversations With God

7 Keys to Intimacy With Jesus

Go Into All the World

You can find my published books on my Amazon author page here:

http://tinyurl.com/jq3h893.

About the Author

Matthew Robert Payne grew up in a Baptist church and gave his life to Jesus Christ at the tender age of 8. At 14, he was sexually abused on a beach, which negatively affected his sexuality and his identity for many years as he fell into a life of sexual addiction.

Matthew started to hear Jesus speak at age 14. After struggling with sexual addiction for 25 years, he came back into the arms of Christ and started to prophesy over people. Matthew estimates that he has given about 20,000 personal prophecies or messages from Jesus to people. A person that is not a Christian would say that this gift is similar to a reading.

Matthew is not perfect yet and freely admits that he has not conquered all of the sin in his life. However, he is very obedient and does what God tells him to do. Yes, that is right! God speaks to Matthew and through him.

It is his hope that if you liked this book, that you might explore other Christian books that he has written, most of which are fairly inexpensive in the Kindle format. Michael mentioned some of the best books for people during this interview.